70 THOUSAND, MILLION, MILLION, MILLION STARS IN SPACE

PAUL ROCKETT

Perspectives is published by Raintree, Chicago, Illinois, www.capstonepub.com

Library of Congress Cataloging-in-Publication Data
Rockett, Paul, author.
 70 thousand, million, million, million stars in space / Paul Rockett.
     pages cm.—(The big countdown)
 Summary: "You can count numbers all around you, from the eight legs on a spider to the one nose on your face. But can you count the stars in the sky? Explore space, from galaxies and stars to the planets in our solar system, including Earth and the Moon."—Provided by publisher.
 Includes bibliographical references and index.
 ISBN 978-1-4109-6875-3 (library binding)
 ISBN 978-1-4109-6882-1 (paperback)
 ISBN 978-1-4109-6896-8 (ebook PDF)
1. Astronomy—Juvenile literature.
2. Outer space—Juvenile literature.
3. Universe—Juvenile literature.
I. Title. II. Title: Seventy thousand, million, million, million stars in space.

 QB46.R58 2016
 520.2—dc23   2014025331

Author: Paul Rockett
Illustrator: Mark Ruffle

Originally published in 2014 by Franklin Watts.
Copyright © Franklin Watts 2014.
Franklin Watts is a division of Hachette Children's Books, a Hachette UK company.
www.hachette.co.uk

Printed in China.

Picture credits: Art Archive/Alamy: 22t; Marcel Clemens/Shutterstock: 11t; ESA/Hubble/NASA: 9tr; Peter Horree/Alamy: 21tr; Hubble data: NASA, ESA and A.Zeus ; GALEX data: NASA, JPL-CALech, GALEX Team, J.Huchra et al ; Spitzer data: NASA/JPL/CAltech/S. Willner. All Harvard-Smithsonian Center for Astrophysics: 9tl; Iryna1/Shutterstock: 21cl; Panos Karas/Shutterstock: 20tr; NASA/JPL/Caltech: 9tc; NASA/JPL/Space Science Institute: 16tr; Nicku/Shutterstock: 20bl, 20br, 21cr; Charles O'Rear/Corbis: 7bl; Vadim Petrakov/Shuttterstock: 23bl; Photo Researchers/Alamy: 21br; Subaru/NASA/JPL-Caltech: 4tl.

Throughout the book you are given data relating to various pieces of information covering the topic. The numbers will most likely be an estimation based on research made over a period of time and in a particular area. Some other research may reach a different set of data, and all these figures may change with time as new research and information is gathered. The numbers provided within this book are believed to be correct at the time of printing.

THE BIG COUNTDOWN
70 THOUSAND, MILLION, MILLION, MILLION STARS IN SPACE

CONTENTS

COUNTING DOWN THE UNIVERSE	4
70 THOUSAND, MILLION, MILLION, MILLION STARS IN SPACE	6
THERE ARE 500 BILLION GALAXIES IN THE UNIVERSE	8
THE MILKY WAY IS 13.2 BILLION YEARS OLD	10
HOW WIDE IS OUR SOLAR SYSTEM?	12
500 MILLION PEOPLE WATCHED THE FIRST MOON LANDING	14
DO ALIENS LIVE 35.4 MILLION MILES (57 MILLION KM) AWAY?	16
THE SUN IS MILLIONS OF DEGREES HOT	18
1642 DEATH OF GALILEO GALILEI	20
75–76 YEARS FOR AN APPEARANCE OF HALLEY'S COMET	22
27 MOONS OF URANUS	24
24 HOURS FOR EARTH TO ROTATE	26
ONE YEAR FOR EARTH TO ORBIT THE SUN	28
FURTHER INFORMATION AND LARGE NUMBERS	30
GLOSSARY	31
INDEX	32

COUNTING DOWN THE UNIVERSE

The universe contains everything we know and more. It is a size that is so big, it is difficult for us to imagine. However, many astronomers believe that about **14,000,000,000 years ago** the universe was thousands of times smaller than a pinhead. Then this tiny dot suddenly exploded—an event called the big bang. The universe grew from this explosion, and it is still expanding in size today.

WHAT WE CAN OBSERVE

When talking about the universe and all the galaxies, planets, and stars inside it, astronomers are mostly talking about the "observable universe." This consists of everything that can be detected by modern technology. We may be unable to see or count any objects beyond the observable universe, but we know that the following exists within it:

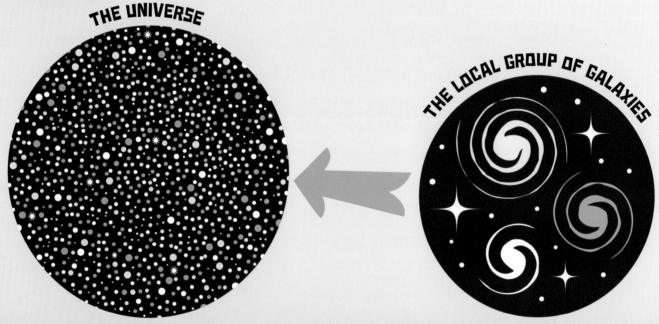

THE UNIVERSE

THE LOCAL GROUP OF GALAXIES

MEASURING THE UNIVERSE

Astronomers use light travel to measure how far away things are in space. Light is incredibly fast—it can travel about seven times around Earth in one second!

One light-year = 5,879,000,000,000 miles (9.4 trillion km)
One light-month = 482,843,000,000 miles (777 billion km)
One light-week = 112,655,000,000 miles (181.3 billion km)
One light-day = 16,094,000,000 miles (25.9 billion km)
One light-hour = 671,081,000 miles (1.08 billion km)
One light-minute = 11,177,000 miles (18 million km)
One light-second = 186,282 miles (299,792 km)

VIEWING THE UNIVERSE

The pollution from large cities and industrialization makes it difficult for us to get a clear view of the stars and planets in the night sky.
This was not such a problem for astronomers in the past, who began mapping the universe from what they could see with the naked eye.

In the 1600s, the invention of the telescope meant that astronomers could see three to four times farther into space.

Today, astronomers view the universe through large observatories and study computer data collected from satellites and space missions out in the solar system.

HYDRA

CRUX

CONSTELLATIONS

Some of the stars in the night sky are grouped into constellations. There are **88 constellations**. They are formations of stars that join up like a dot-to-dot puzzle to look like a creature or an object.

Constellations are often used as a way of mapping the sky, helping sailors to navigate at night. The largest constellation is Hydra; it is made up of **16 main stars** and is said to represent a water snake. The smallest constellation is the Crux or Southern Cross. This is made up of **four stars**.

THE MILKY WAY

OUR SOLAR SYSTEM

EARTH

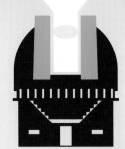

Measurements of light travel are categorized into periods of time:
one light-year is the measurement of how fast light can travel within one year.

(five trillion, eight hundred seventy-nine billion)
(four hundred eighty-two billion, eight hundred forty-three million)
(one hundred twelve billion, six hundred fifty-five million)
(sixteen billion, ninety-four million)
(six hundred seventy-one million, eighty-one thousand)
(eleven million, one hundred seventy-seven thousand)
(one hundred eighty-six thousand, two hundred eighty-two)

A scientist once said: "The total number of stars in the universe is larger than all the grains of sand on all the beaches of the planet Earth."

The number of stars in space and the number of grains of sand on Earth can only be estimated. An advanced telescope can count the stars within a small area of our galaxy. This number can then be multiplied by the size of our galaxy, which can then be multiplied by the number of galaxies within the universe, providing an estimate of the number of stars in space.

THERE ARE 70 THOUSAND, MILLION, MILLION, MILLION STARS IN THE UNIVERSE.

This number can also be written as 70 sextillion, and when written in numerals it looks like this:

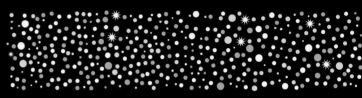

70,000,000,000,000,000,000,000

THERE ARE SEVEN THOUSAND FIVE HUNDRED MILLION, MILLION, MILLION GRAINS OF SAND ON THE PLANET EARTH.

This number can also be written as seven quintillion, five hundred quadrillion, and when written in numerals it looks like this:

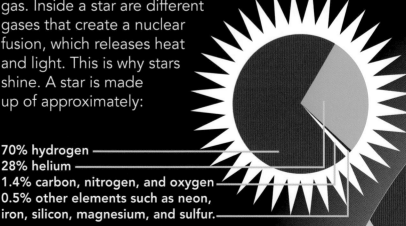

7,500,000,000,000,000,000

ESTIMATES

Estimates are not exact amounts, but are educated guesses based on the best information available. Not all galaxies are the same, so the final number of stars is unlikely to be correct.

WHAT IS A STAR?

A star is a ball of hot, glowing gas. Inside a star are different gases that create a nuclear fusion, which releases heat and light. This is why stars shine. A star is made up of approximately:

70% hydrogen
28% helium
1.4% carbon, nitrogen, and oxygen
0.5% other elements such as neon, iron, silicon, magnesium, and sulfur.

IS THAT A STAR IN THE SKY?

Apart from the Sun, the closest star to Earth is **Proxima Centauri**, which is over **24 trillion miles** (40 trillion km) away.

The **Sun** is a star at the center of our solar system. Its distance from Earth depends on Earth's position while orbiting the Sun. On average, it is **93 million miles** (150 million km) away.

Venus' distance from Earth varies depending on the orbit of both planets. Venus can be as close as **23,612,105 miles** (38 million km) or as far away as **162,177,881 miles** (261 million km). At its nearest point, Venus can be seen in the night sky. It reflects sunlight, making it look like a very bright star.

The **Moon** is visible at night because it reflects sunlight. The average distance between Earth and the Moon is **238,857 miles** (384,403 km).

A **comet** is not a star. It is formed by bits of dust and gas that collect into an icy form. Comets take their name from the Greek *aster kometes*, which means "long-haired stars." Comets have come as close to Earth as **31,068,560 miles** (50 million km).

Asteroids are not stars. They are bits of rock that have not managed to come together as large planets. In 2013, an asteroid came within **17,200 miles** (27,680 km) of Earth.

A **meteor** is a piece of space rock that enters Earth's atmosphere. As it falls it begins to burn and becomes a fireball. Fiery falling meteors can look very similar to fireworks, which has led them to be called "shooting stars" even though they are not stars.

Usually a meteor burns out into nothing as it heads toward Earth, but sometimes meteors do collide with Earth. A meteor that hits Earth is called a meteorite.

This crater, in the Arizona desert, was caused by a meteorite.

THERE ARE 500 BILLION
GALAXIES IN THE UNIVERSE

> **The largest structures in the universe are galaxy superclusters.** These contain millions of galaxies and can measure hundreds of millions of light-years across.

Smaller groups of galaxies are called clusters.

Galaxies are collections of stars that are drawn to a common center of gravity. Some are small with only a few million stars, while others could have as many as **400,000,000,000 stars** or more. Some scientists estimate that there are around **500,000,000,000 galaxies** in the universe.

Most galaxies are gathered together in small clusters. Our galaxy, the Milky Way, is part of a cluster of galaxies called the Local Group.

There are about **30 galaxies** within the Local Group. The three largest are:

ANDROMEDA
2,500,000 **light-years** from Earth

MILKY WAY
Our galaxy

TRIANGULUM
3,000,000 light-years from Earth

How many stars in each galaxy?

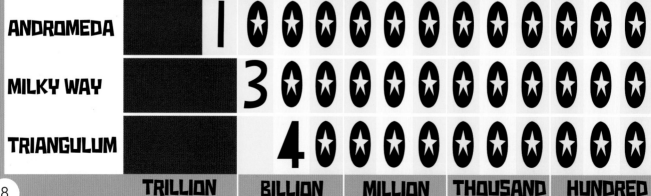

	TRILLION	BILLION	MILLION	THOUSAND	HUNDRED
ANDROMEDA		1 0 0 0 0 0	0 0 0	0 0	0 0
MILKY WAY		3 0 0 0 0	0 0 0	0 0	0 0
TRIANGULUM		4 0 0 0	0 0 0	0 0	0 0

DIFFERENT GALAXIES

There are **three kinds of galaxies**. The only difference between them is their shape.

SPIRAL

Spiral galaxies have long arms that come out from the center. New stars are created in the arms, with large stars causing the dust clouds around them to glow brightly. The three largest galaxies in the Local Group are spiral.

ELLIPTICAL

The stars within an elliptical galaxy are often very close together, which can make the center look like one giant star. New stars are not created in this galaxy. The stars it contains were created a very long time ago.

IRREGULAR

Any galaxy that doesn't look like a spiral or elliptical galaxy is categorized as an irregular galaxy.

MOVEMENT

All galaxies move through space.

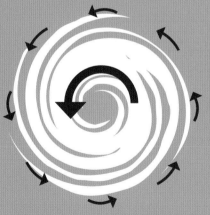

They rotate around their center with the speed of movement becoming slower as the galaxy material extends and spreads outward.

A cluster of galaxies also rotates around a central point of gravity within that cluster.

GRAVITY

All the stars in a galaxy are kept together by the gravity of other stars and the gravity that is at the center of each galaxy and cluster of galaxies.

Gravity is a force that attracts one object to another object. The movement of galaxies, planets, and moons in space is due to their interaction with the gravitational pull from other objects. It is this force that holds the galaxies together, and the force that keeps planets and moons in their orbits.

THE MILKY WAY IS
13.2 BILLION YEARS OLD

The Milky Way is the galaxy that contains our solar system.

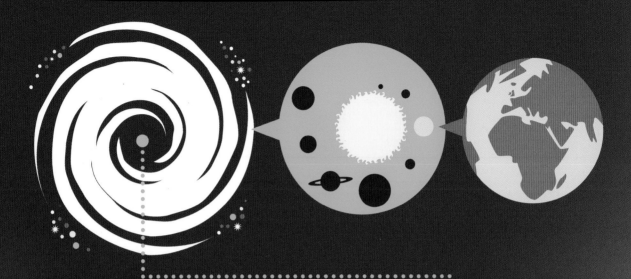

Some scientists believe the Milky Way to be as old as the universe itself, whereas our solar system and planet Earth are much younger.

The Milky Way became its current size by eating other galaxies.

MILKY WAY

EARTH

Billions of years old

14 13 12 11 10 9 8 7 6 5 4 3 2 1 0

5%

Less than **5%** of the stars in the Milky Way are brighter or bigger than the Sun.

27,000 LIGHT-YEARS

At the center of the Milky Way is a giant black hole. It is estimated to be **27,000 light-years** from Earth and is four times bigger than the Sun. A black hole has an extremely powerful force of gravity that pulls everything toward it. Even light gets sucked in.

WHERE DID THE MILKY WAY COME FROM?

There are uncertainties about how the Milky Way was formed. A lot of scientists think that during the big bang, collections of gas and dust came together, forming clusters that became galaxies.

Because we are inside the galaxy, we do not see it from Earth as a spiral, but as a thin band arching across the night sky. It appears as a pale, white glow, a sight that has led to the creation of many myths around its origin.

IN ROMAN, GREEK, AND EGYPTIAN MYTHOLOGY,
the Milky Way is believed to have formed from spilled milk.

THE KHOISAN PEOPLE from
southern Africa believe that a young girl who wanted to visit people at night threw up embers from a fire into the sky to light her journey. This created the Milky Way.

IN ARMENIAN MYTHOLOGY,
the Milky Way is called the Straw Thief's Way. The god Vahagn stole some straw and fled across the heavens dropping bits along the way, which created the Milky Way.

AN ANCIENT HINDU story
sees all of the stars and planets above Earth as moving through space like a dolphin. The Milky Way forms the stomach of the dolphin.

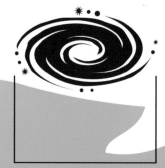

621,371,192,237,333,888 miles (1 quintillion km)

HOW WIDE IS OUR SOLAR SYSTEM?

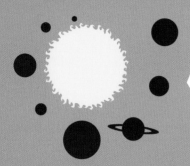

Our solar system is
6,835,083,115 miles wide.

In our solar system there are eight planets orbiting around the Sun.

MERCURY ······ ● ···· 36,039,529 miles (58 million km), 3.22 light-minutes from the Sun

VENUS ·········· ············ 67,108,089 miles (108 million km), 6.01 light-minutes

EARTH ········· ··········· 93,205,679 miles (150 million km), 8.32 light-minutes

MARS ········· ········ 141,672,632 miles (228 million km), 12.7 light-minutes

JUPITER ········· ················· 483,000,000 miles (778 million km), 43.3 light-minutes

SATURN ·······

URANUS ·········

NEPTUNE ·········

The Sun's circumference is about **2,713,411.8 miles** (4,366,813 km).

Earth may seem large, but when we compare it to other objects in our solar system, it is really quite small. The circumference of the eight planets is shown below.

MERCURY · 9,525 miles (15,329 km)

VENUS · 23,628 miles (38,025 km)

EARTH · 24,901 miles (40,075 km)

MARS · 13,263 miles (21,344 km)

JUPITER 279,120 miles (449,200 km)

SATURN 235,301 miles (378,680 km)

URANUS 99,786 miles (160,590 km)

NEPTUNE 96,685 miles (155,600 km)

We could fit **1,000** Earths inside Jupiter.
We could fit **1,000** Jupiters inside the Sun.
It would take **1,000,000** Earths to fill the Sun!

. . . . 888,560,805 miles (1.4 billion km), 1.32 light-hours

. . . . 1,789,549,034 miles (2.8 billion km), 2.66 light-hours

. . . . 2,796,170,365 miles (4.5 billion km), 4.16 light-hours . . . .

500 MILLION PEOPLE WATCHED THE FIRST MOON LANDING

Explorations into space have enabled scientists to learn a lot about Earth's environment and have put satellites into space that allow us to communicate across the world with computers and phones. Astronauts have also gone into space to explore the possibility of humans living on the Moon and on other planets, as well as in space stations.

On July 20, 1969, lunar module *Eagle* (a spacecraft used during the Apollo 11 mission) landed on the Moon. This was the first manned mission to the Moon, and it was broadcast live on TV.

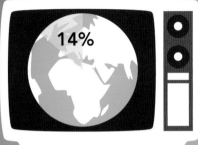

14%

An estimated **500,000,000 people** worldwide watched this event. That's around **14% of the total population** of the world at that time.

MISSIONS TO THE MOON

There have been **45 missions** to the Moon. Of these, only **19** landed successfully. The remaining **26** were either planned crash landings or didn't quite make it in one piece.

Only **six** of the missions to the Moon were manned.

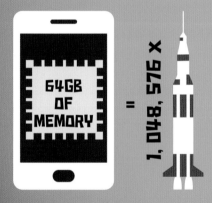

64GB OF MEMORY = x 1,048,576

Apollo 11 computer power

The Apollo Guidance Computer (AGC) that was used to control Apollo 11's modules had approximately **64 KB** of memory. Today's average cell phone has far more computing power.

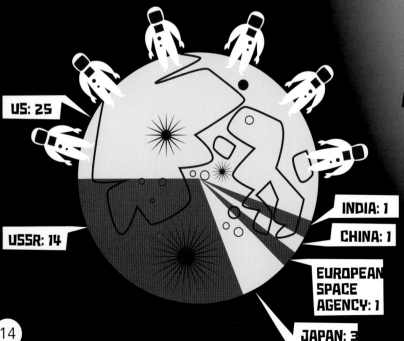

US: 25

USSR: 14

INDIA: 1

CHINA: 1

EUROPEAN SPACE AGENCY: 1

JAPAN: 3

WHERE DID THEY LAND?

Apollo 16
Landed here:
April 27, 1972

Apollo 17
Landed here:
December 11,
1972

Apollo 12
Landed here:
November 24,
1969

Apollo 15
Landed here:
August 7,
1971

Apollo 14
Landed here:
February 5,
1971

Apollo 11
Landed here:
July 20, 1969

12
Number of people to have walked on the Moon.

530
Number of people to have gone into space.

No animal has been on the Moon, but many different creatures have been sent into space. These include: monkeys, pigs, dogs, cats, guinea pigs, mice, rats, frogs, jellyfish, tortoises, snails, and fruit flies.

DO ALIENS LIVE 35.4 MILLION MILES (57 MILLION KM) AWAY?

There is no scientific evidence to prove the existence of aliens. However, there are some scientists who believe that aliens may live **35,400,000 miles** (57 million km) away on Enceladus, one of Saturn's moons.

ENCELADUS

Unlike many planets and moons, Enceladus contains elements that are suitable for life, such as flowing water geysers and a source of heat.

13 feet (4m)

9.8 feet (3 m)

6.5 feet (2m)

However, **one in five** people believes that alien life-forms are much closer and are walking among us, in disguise. There are varying reports of what aliens look like.

REPORTED DESCRIPTIONS OF ALIENS

3.2 feet (1m)

A 13-FOOT-TALL (4M) HUMANOID

with a blood-red face; large, greenish-orange eyes; and three-fingered hands.

A 6.5-FOOT-TALL (2M) LIGHTWEIGHT HUMANOID with a narrow, elegant body; a large head; large eyes; small nose, mouth, and ears; delicate, five-fingered hands; all portions of the head and body covered with a soft, downy, neat fur.

UFOs

UFOs (unidentified flying objects) are believed to be alien vehicles from outer space. What a lot of people think of as UFOs usually turn out to be lights from vehicles, birds, or odd-shaped clouds. However, a study into UFO sightings in the United States between 1951 and 1954 found that out of 3,201 sightings, 704 remained unidentified.

Results of investigations into UFO sightings:

1.0% birds

2% psychological

2.2% light phenomena

0.4% clouds

5% other

22% unknown origin (UFOs)

9% insufficient information

15% balloons

22% astronomical (stars and planets)

22% aircraft

A 5-FOOT-TALL (1.5 M) HUMANOID with a large, bald head; small, sunken eyes; small, concave nose with two nostrils; thin, lipless mouth devoid of teeth; and an ear hole on each side of the head with a tiny lobe. The longest part of the arm is between the elbow and the wrist, and the hand has four long, slender fingers with a suction pad on the end of each one.

THE MOST POPULAR DESCRIPTIONS FOR UFOS ARE:

1. Lights
2. Triangles
3. Circles

A 3-FOOT-TALL (90 CM) HUMANOID with a large, hairless, earthy-green-skinned head; large, yellow-green, hemispherical, protruding eyes with vertical pupils; no eyebrows or eye lashes; and ring-like, yellow-green eyelids at the base of the eye. The face has a large, long, straight nose. The mouth is a slit and continually opens and closes like a fish's mouth. The hands each have eight jointless, green fingers.

The Sun is at the center of our solar system.
It is the largest star in our solar system, and like other stars, it generates its heat through nuclear fusion in its core. The heat and light that come from the Sun are essential for life on Earth. The Sun provides energy for plants, and plants provide food for many animals.

CORE
27,000,032°F (15,000,000°C)

RADIOACTIVE ZONE
The energy generated from the core takes 170,000 years to travel through this area.

PHOTOSPHERE
9,941°F (5,505°C)
The photosphere is the surface of the Sun, although there are two further layers of gas that are above it: the chromosphere and the corona.

SUNSPOTS
These are cooler spots on the Sun, which is why they appear darker.

SOLAR FLARES
These are explosions on the surface of the Sun that occur when a big buildup of energy is released.

170,000 YEARS

Most of the visible light from the Sun comes from the fact that it is hot.

HOW CLOSE CAN WE GET?

The better your protective clothing or equipment, the closer you can get to the Sun without being harmed. Some scientists believe that a spacecraft could get as close as **1,300,000 miles** (2,092,147 km) to the Sun. In a specially designed spacesuit, an astronaut could get as close as **3,000,000 miles** (4,828,032 km) but would not survive for long before dying from the heat.

3,000,000 miles
(4,828,032 km)

2,999,999.4 miles
(4,828,031 km)

1,299,999.3 miles
(2,092,146 km)

1,300,000 miles
(2,092,147 km)

2,485,485 miles
(4,000,000 km)

3,106,856 miles
(5,000,000 km)

1,242,742 miles
(2,000,000 km)

1,864,114 miles
(3,000,000 km)

621,371 miles
(1,000,000 km)

DO NOT LOOK DIRECTLY INTO THE SUN!

Looking directly into the Sun will damage your eyesight and could cause permanent blindness. Do not look into the Sun when wearing sunglasses because they don't offer sufficient protection. You should use specially designed solar binoculars or eclipse glasses that are fitted with solar filters.

The temperature at Earth's core is **9,806°F** (5,430°C)—not too far off from the temperature on the Sun's surface.

The average temperature of Earth's surface is **57.2°F** (14°C).

The hottest places on Earth are the deserts near the equator, reaching up to **135.86°F** (57.7°C).

The coldest place on Earth is near the South Pole at **−128.2°F** (−89°C).

The Sun's heat decreases the farther you travel to the outer limits of our solar system.

900°F (482°C)

800°F (427°C)

140°F (60°C)

40°F (4°C)

−160°F (−107°C)

−330°F (−201°C)

Venus

Mercury

Earth

Mars

Jupiter

Saturn

Uranus

Neptune

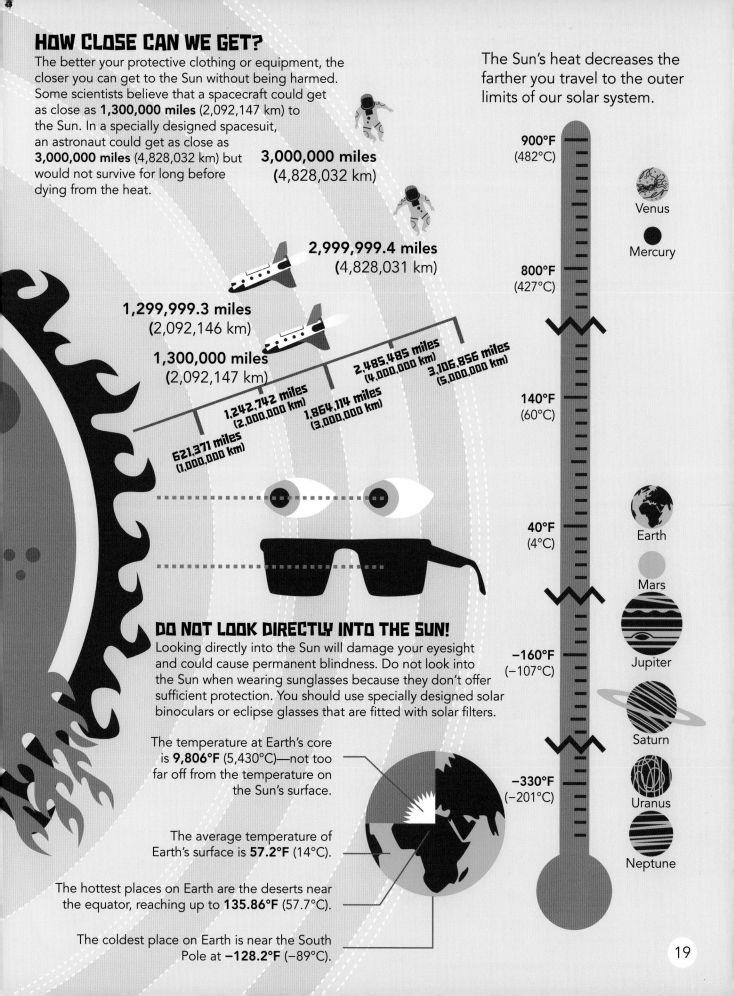

1642 DEATH OF GALILEO GALILEI

Galileo Galilei died under house arrest because of his revolutionary scientific discoveries about space. Here are a few other astronomers who have studied the stars.

The belief that all planets in our solar system orbit the Sun is called heliocentric. This is the model of the universe that Galilei supported.

The belief that Earth is at the center of our solar system, around which the Sun and planets orbit, is called geocentric.

ARISTOTLE 384 BC–322 BC

Aristotle proved that Earth is spherical. He pointed out that during a lunar eclipse, the shadow of Earth across the Moon is always circular, proving Earth to be round. An eclipse is when an object hides our view of another object. In a lunar eclipse, this is Earth's shadow limiting what we can see of the Moon.

Aristotle also pointed out that as you travel further north or south, the positions of the stars in the sky change. There are constellations visible in the north that you cannot see in the south and vice versa.

SUN — EARTH — MOON

LUNAR ECLIPSE

JOHANNES KEPLER 1571–1630

It had been thought that the planets followed a perfectly circular orbit around the Sun, but Kepler discovered that their orbital paths are actually elliptical.

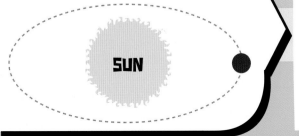

SUN

ISAAC NEWTON 1643–1727

Newton suggested that the force that keeps things in place and pulls things together is gravity. This is why apples fall to the ground and why Earth orbits the Sun.

Newton proved that the force of gravity is stronger the greater the mass of the object, which is one of the reasons why the Moon orbits Earth and not the other way around. Before Newton proved this, it was believed that the planets were held in place by an invisible shield. He also created a mathematical model that accurately predicts the movements of planetary objects.

CLAUDIUS PTOLEMY 90–168

Ptolemy accepted the geocentric model of the solar system but believed that the planets revolved around a further circle than that of their main orbit. He also established the order of the solar system that was almost correct.

| Earth | Moon | Mercury | Venus | Sun | Mars | Jupiter | Saturn |

NICOLAUS COPERNICUS 1473–1543

In 1542 Copernicus published a book called *On the Revolutions of the Celestial Spheres* arguing that the Sun, not Earth, is at the center of the universe. This established the heliocentric universe (*helios* being the Greek word for "Sun").

GALILEO GALILEI 1564–1642

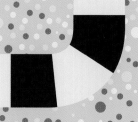

Galilei built one of the first telescopes and made many astronomical discoveries, including the large moons of Jupiter, sunspots on the Sun, and mountains and valleys on the surface of the Moon.

Galilei supported Copernicus' belief in a heliocentric universe. However, whereas Copernicus only received mild objections to his system, the Catholic Church imprisoned Galilei for supporting it. He died while under house arrest.

ALBERT EINSTEIN 1879–1955

Einstein viewed the universe as held within space-time. Space-time is like a stretched rubber sheet that is warped by large objects positioned on it, like the Sun and the planets. These objects cause space-time to bend. This bend is felt as gravity. Einstein proved that light bends in the presence of a large gravitational field such as around this bend within space-time. He also proved that time goes more slowly in areas with low gravity, where there is less of a bend.

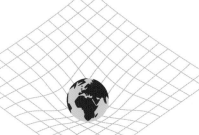

75–76 YEARS FOR AN APPEARANCE OF HALLEY'S COMET

Comets are balls of ice, rock, and dust that go around the Sun in a highly elliptical orbit. They go to the outer reaches of our solar system and can take from **3** to **1,000 years** to complete their orbit.

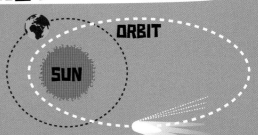
ORBIT

SUN

Halley's comet is named after Edmond Halley.

Edmond Halley was the first person to demonstrate the periodic return of a comet. He proposed that a comet sighted in 1531 was the same comet that had appeared in 1607 and again in 1682. He predicted that this comet would return in 1759. His prediction was correct.

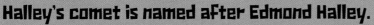
1531   **1607**   **1682** **1759**

HAROLD

In fact, the appearance of Halley's comet has been traced much further back through history, with one possible sighting recorded in a Chinese chronicle dating from 240 BC. It is also recorded on the Bayeaux Tapestry from 1066.

BAD OMENS

Comets have at times been considered as bad omens, warning of terrible times ahead.

COMET SEEN IN 1347
Outbreak of the Black Death around the world, killing over **25,000,000** people.

COMET SEEN IN 1066
King Harold II died at the Battle of Hastings with the Norman-French gaining the rule of England. This is the comet that appears on the Bayeaux Tapestry.

COMET SEEN IN AD 79
The eruption of the volcano Vesuvius that wiped out the city of Pompeii in Italy.

COMET SEEN IN AD 70
The Siege of Jerusalem, where the Roman army invaded, causing mass destruction to the city.

HALLEY'S COMET
can be seen from Earth for roughly **five months**, although this depends on local pollution levels. For a large portion of this time, it is only visible from the Southern Hemisphere. It also spends a lot of this time very near to the Sun, so that viewing it with the naked eye is nearly impossible.

Halley's comet returns every **75–76 years**. It will next be visible in our sky in 2061.

SOUTHERN HEMISPHERE

Comets are sometimes referred to as "dirty snowballs." The amount of dirt, rock, and gravel compacted by ice makes it look like the kind of snowball you don't want thrown at you.

ANATOMY OF A COMET

A comet speeds up the nearer it gets to the Sun. The combination of increased sunlight and speed causes parts of the comet to fragment, creating **two tails**: a dust tail and a gas tail. The tails can stretch out for **millions of miles**.

As a comet gets nearer to the Sun, it develops an atmosphere around it, which is called a coma. The coma can grow to become **thousands of miles** in diameter.

A main part of a comet is the nucleus, which is the compacted rock, dust, and ice. The nucleus may only be a **few miles** wide.

Like the Moon, a comet is made visible by reflecting the light from the Sun.

Some scientists believe that comets brought water to Earth, allowing life to begin.

GAS TAIL

DUST TAIL

COMA

Comets are roughly the size of a small town.

NUCLEUS

27 MOONS OF URANUS

What are moons?
Moons are planetary objects that orbit planets. Moons are always smaller in size than the planets they orbit and can be made of similar rocks and gases.

How are moons formed?
There are three different theories as to how moons are formed.

1. Moons are pieces of their planets that have fallen away.

2. Moons are debris created from the impact of two planets colliding.

3. Moons are wandering elements formed from somewhere else in the solar system.

As astronomers are able to see more clearly into space, more moons are discovered. Uranus' **27 moons** have been spotted over a period of **216 years**.

1787	1851	1948	1985	1986	1997	1999	2001	2003

WHILE PLANETS ORBIT THE SUN, MOONS ORBIT THE PLANETS

Planets	Number of moons
Mercury	●
Venus	
Earth	🌍 ꞈ
Mars	ꞈꞈ
Jupiter	(many moons)
Saturn	(many moons)
Uranus	(many moons)
Neptune	ꞈꞈꞈ

MOONS ARE ALSO KNOWN AS NATURAL SATELLITES
Moons are not to be confused with the mechanical satellites that are put into space to transmit communication back to Earth.

180

8,000

There are approximately **180** natural satellites in our solar system and **8,000** communication satellites.

OUR MOON

The Moon does not produce light of its own but reflects the light from the Sun.

The Sun only lights up the half of the Moon that faces toward it.

The side of the Moon that we never see is called the far or dark side of the Moon.

PHASES OF THE MOON

As the Moon moves around Earth, we see different parts of the half that is lit by the Sun. The different shapes that we see are called phases. There are **eight phases**, all with different names.

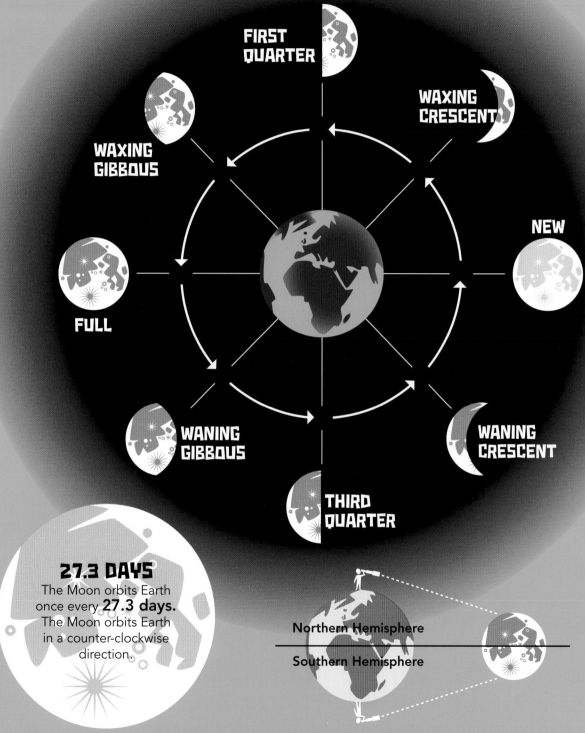

FIRST QUARTER

WAXING CRESCENT

WAXING GIBBOUS

NEW

FULL

WANING GIBBOUS

WANING CRESCENT

THIRD QUARTER

27.3 DAYS
The Moon orbits Earth once every **27.3 days.** The Moon orbits Earth in a counter-clockwise direction.

Northern Hemisphere

Southern Hemisphere

The Moon also takes **27.3 days** to spin around once on its axis, which means that the same side of the Moon always faces Earth. However, in the Southern Hemisphere the Moon is seen upside down to the view seen in the Northern Hemisphere.

24 HOURS FOR EARTH TO ROTATE

Earth moves in two ways: it travels in orbit around the Sun and it rotates on its axis. It takes 24 hours to rotate on its axis.

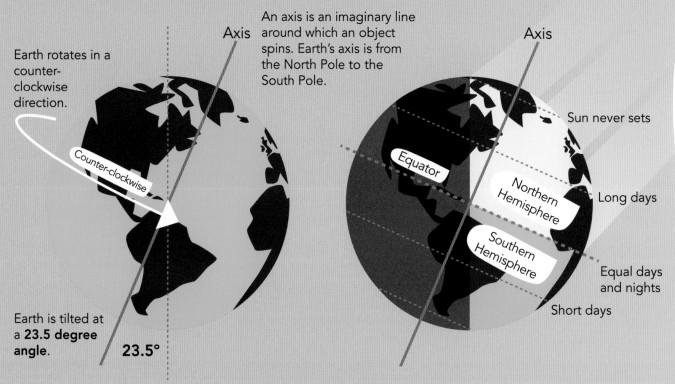

Axis

An axis is an imaginary line around which an object spins. Earth's axis is from the North Pole to the South Pole.

Earth rotates in a counter-clockwise direction.

Counter-clockwise

Earth is tilted at a **23.5 degree angle**.

23.5°

Axis

Sun never sets

Equator

Northern Hemisphere

Long days

Southern Hemisphere

Equal days and nights

Short days

The part facing toward the Sun is in daylight while the part facing away from the Sun is in darkness. This means that when the Northern Hemisphere is tilted toward the Sun, places in this hemisphere get more than **12 hours** of daylight, while places in the Southern Hemisphere are tilted away from the Sun and get less than **12 hours** of daylight. On the equator there are always **12 hours** of daylight.

EAST

WEST

THE SUN RISES TOWARD THE EAST AND SETS TOWARD THE WEST.
During the day it appears to follow a curved path across the sky. This apparent movement is not caused by the movement of the Sun, but by Earth spinning on its axis.

There are two ways of reading the time it takes Earth to rotate on its axis. One is a solar day, and the other a sidereal day.

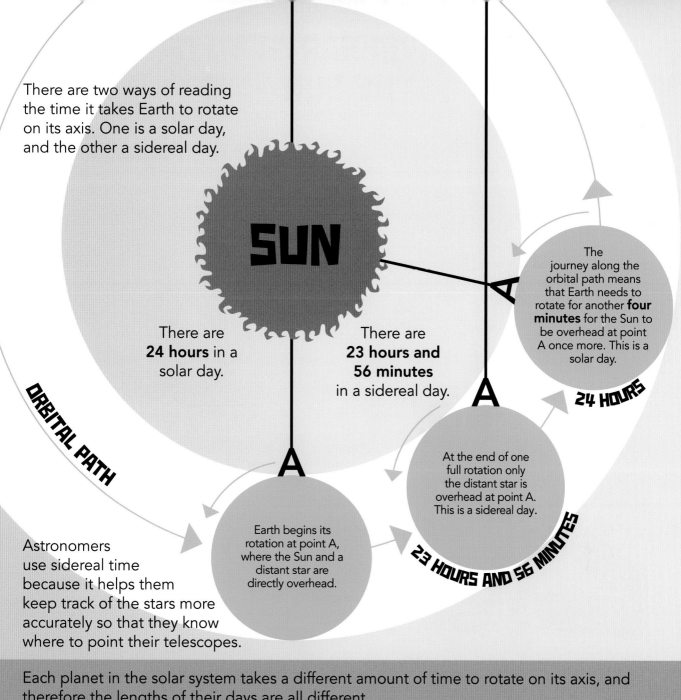

SUN

ORBITAL PATH

There are **24 hours** in a solar day.

There are **23 hours and 56 minutes** in a sidereal day.

The journey along the orbital path means that Earth needs to rotate for another **four minutes** for the Sun to be overhead at point A once more. This is a solar day.

24 HOURS

A

At the end of one full rotation only the distant star is overhead at point A. This is a sidereal day.

23 HOURS AND 56 MINUTES

A

Earth begins its rotation at point A, where the Sun and a distant star are directly overhead.

Astronomers use sidereal time because it helps them keep track of the stars more accurately so that they know where to point their telescopes.

Each planet in the solar system takes a different amount of time to rotate on its axis, and therefore the lengths of their days are all different.

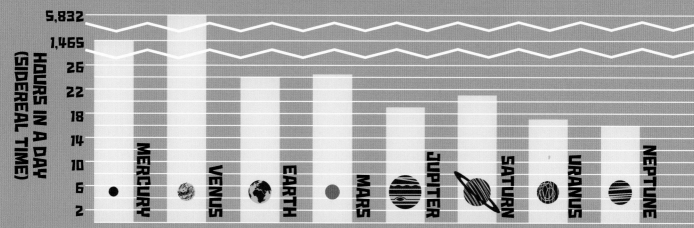

HOURS IN A DAY (SIDEREAL TIME)

5,832
1,465
26
22
18
14
10
6
2

MERCURY VENUS EARTH MARS JUPITER SATURN URANUS NEPTUNE

ONE YEAR FOR EARTH TO ORBIT THE SUN

One year = 365 days
Or does it?
Although we say that Earth takes one year to orbit the Sun, it actually takes **365.25** days.

The **.25 day** (quarter of a day) means that every **four years** there is an extra day, and so rather than **365 days**, that year has **366 days**. It is known as a leap year and falls on **February 29**.

There is a **1** in **1,461** chance of being born on

February 29.

People born on a leap day are called **leaplings**.

Leaplings have to wait four years before they can "officially" celebrate their birthdays.

I am 3

I am 15

Born February 29

Born February 28

In some countries it was a tradition that women could only propose to men on a leap day.

Orbiting speeds The Milky Way, the solar system, and Earth all travel at different speeds.

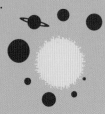

671,081 miles/h (1,080,000 km/h)

514,495 miles/h (828,000 km/h)

67,108 miles/h (108,000 km/h)

Speed of a cheetah **70 miles/h** (112.65 km/h)

EARTH TRAVELS 584 MILLION MILES (940 MILLION KM) IN ONE ORBIT

To travel the same distance that Earth covers in one orbit, you would have to walk the distance between Scotland and Australia **64,661 times** or New York and Australia **56,674 times**.

x 64,661

x 55,674

Earth's orbit around the Sun is elliptical, so the distance between Earth and the Sun varies throughout the year.

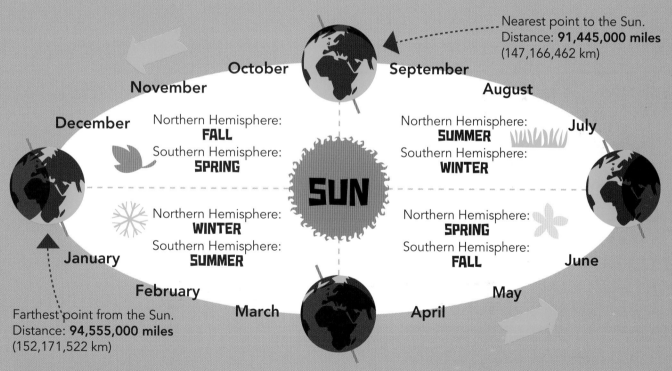

October

November

December

September

August

July

Nearest point to the Sun.
Distance: **91,445,000 miles**
(147,166,462 km)

Northern Hemisphere:
FALL
Southern Hemisphere:
SPRING

Northern Hemisphere:
SUMMER
Southern Hemisphere:
WINTER

SUN

Northern Hemisphere:
WINTER
Southern Hemisphere:
SUMMER

Northern Hemisphere:
SPRING
Southern Hemisphere:
FALL

January

February

March

April

May

June

Farthest point from the Sun.
Distance: **94,555,000 miles**
(152,171,522 km)

FOUR SEASONS

The change in temperature and sunlight that each season experiences is caused by the tilt on Earth's axis as it rotates and travels along its orbit around the Sun.

When the Northern Hemisphere is tilted away from the Sun, it is winter in this hemisphere and summer in the Southern Hemisphere. So while the Northern Hemisphere is having summer, fall, winter, and spring, the Southern Hemisphere is having the opposite: winter, spring, summer, and fall.

FURTHER INFORMATION

BOOKS
Know It All: Space by Andrew Langley (Franklin Watts, 2013)
The Real Scientist: Space! by Peter Riley (Franklin Watts, 2012)
Science F.A.Q.: Why Are Black Holes Black? by Thomas Canavan
(Franklin Watts, 2013)
The World of Infographics: Space by Jon Richards and Ed Simkins
(Wayland, 2012)

WEBSITES
BBC Newsround's website containing great videos, news, facts, and
quizzes:
www.bbc.co.uk/newsround/14082427
NASA's website for kids, containing games, videos, and pictures:
www.nasa.gov/audience/forkids/kidsclub/flash/index.html
Quizzes and fact files on space:
www.sciencekids.co.nz/space.html

Note to parents and teachers:
Every effort has been made by the publisher to ensure that these websites contain no
inappropriate or offensive material. However, because of the nature of the Internet, it is
impossible to guarantee that the content of these sites will not be altered. We strongly
advise that Internet access is supervised by a responsible adult.

LARGE NUMBERS
1,000,000,000,000,000,000,000,000,000,000,000 = ONE DECILLION
1,000,000,000,000,000,000,000,000,000,000 = ONE NONILLION
1,000,000,000,000,000,000,000,000,000 = ONE OCTILLION
1,000,000,000,000,000,000,000,000 = ONE SEPTILLION
1,000,000,000,000,000,000,000 = ONE SEXTILLION
1,000,000,000,000,000,000 = ONE QUINTILLION
1,000,000,000,000,000 = ONE QUADRILLION
1,000,000,000,000 = ONE TRILLION
1,000,000,000 = ONE BILLION
1,000,000 = ONE MILLION
1,000 = ONE THOUSAND
100 = ONE HUNDRED
10 = TEN
1 = ONE

alien	a creature from another world
asteroid	rocks, smaller than planets, that orbit the Sun
astronaut	a person trained to go into space
astronomer	person who studies the stars
axis	an imaginary line around which a planet rotates
big bang	an explosion that marked the birth of the universe
black hole	an area in space that has a strong gravitational force at its center
cluster	a group of similar objects
comet	object made of ice and dust orbiting around the Sun
constellation	a group of stars
eclipse	the view of an object hidden by another
elliptical	relating to an oval shape
equator	an imaginary line drawn around Earth separating the Northern and Southern Hemispheres
estimate	an approximate calculation
galaxy	a collection of planets and stars held together by gravity
geocentric	belief that Earth is at the center of the solar system
gravity	a force that pulls objects together
heliocentric	belief that the Sun is at the center of the solar system
humanoid	resembling a human
leapling	a person born on February 29, a leap day
meteor	piece of space rock smaller than an asteroid
meteorite	the name for a meteor that has landed on Earth
nuclear fusion	a process where two elements combine to create another element, releasing large amounts of energy
observatory	a building designed to help see into space using telescopes
omen	an occurrence that suggests bad things to come
orbit	a curved path an object follows going around another object
phases	stages of development
phenomena	unusual occurrences
planetary	relating to planets
prediction	a thing told about the future
psychological	relating to the mind and mental activity
radioactive	emissions in response to a nuclear reaction
satellite	an object placed in orbit around a planet
sidereal day	time it takes Earth to make a full rotation in alignment to a distant star
solar day	time it takes Earth to make a rotation in alignment with the Sun
star	a bright, shining ball of gas in the night sky
telescope	an instrument designed to make distant objects appear near
UFO	stands for unidentified flying object, an unexplained object in the sky

INDEX

aliens 16–17
Andromeda 8
Apollo missions 14, 15
Aristotle 20
asteroids 7
astronauts 14, 15, 19
astronomers 4, 5, 20–21, 24, 27

big bang 4, 11

comets 7, 22–23
    Halley's 22
constellations 5, 20
Copernicus, Nicolaus 21
Crux 5

days, sidereal 27
days, solar 26, 27, 28

Earth 4, 6, 7, 8, 10, 11, 12, 13, 14, 18, 19, 20,
    21, 22, 23, 24, 25, 26–29
eclipses 19, 20
Einstein, Albert 21
Enceladus 16
exploration, space 14–15

flares, solar 18
fusion, nuclear 6, 18

galaxies 4, 6, 8–11
    elliptical 9
    irregular 9
    Local Group 4, 8, 9
    spiral 9
Galilei, Galileo 20, 21
gravity 8, 9, 10, 20, 21

Halley, Edmond 22
Hemisphere, Northern 25, 26, 29
Hemisphere, Southern 22, 25, 26, 29
holes, black 10
humanoids 16, 17
Hydra 5

Jupiter 12, 13, 19, 21, 24, 27

Kepler, Johannes 20

leaplings 28
light-years 4, 5, 8, 10

Mars 12, 13, 19, 21, 24, 27
Mercury 12, 13, 19, 21, 24, 27
meteorites 7
meteors 7
Milky Way 5, 8, 10–11, 12, 28
Moon 7, 14–15, 20, 21, 23, 24, 25
    phases of 25
moons 9, 16, 21, 24, 25
myths 11

navigation 5
Neptune 12, 13, 19, 24, 27
Newton, Isaac 20

observatories 5

photosphere 18
planets 4, 5, 7, 9, 11, 12, 13, 14, 16, 17, 19,
    20, 21, 24, 27
Proxima Centauri 7
Ptolemy, Claudius 21

satellites 5, 14, 24
Saturn 12, 13, 16, 19, 21, 24, 27
seasons 29
solar system 5, 7, 10–13, 18–19, 20, 21, 22,
    24, 27, 28
Southern Cross 5
stars 4, 5, 6–9, 10, 11, 17, 18, 20, 27
Sun 7, 10, 12, 13, 18–19, 20, 21, 22, 23, 24,
    25, 26, 27, 28, 29
sunspots 18, 21

telescopes 5, 6, 21, 27
time, sidereal 27
Triangulum 8

UFOs 17
universe, the 4–5, 6, 8, 10, 20, 21
Uranus 12, 13, 19, 24, 27

Venus 7, 12, 13, 19, 21, 24, 27

years 28, 29
    leap 28